9/05

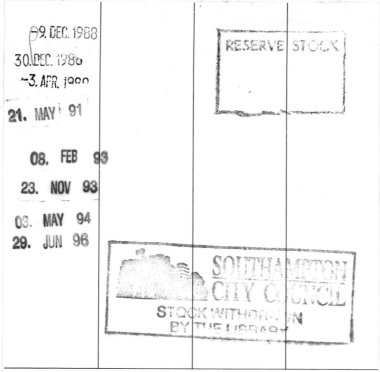

This book is due for return on or before the last date shown above; it may, subject to the book not being reserved by another reader, be renewed by personal application, post, or telephone, quoting this date and details of the book.

HAMPSHIRE COUNTY LIBRARY

Merchant Ships

of the

Solent

Past and Present

Bert Moody

Published By
Kingfisher Railway Productions
65A The Avenue, Southampton SO1 2TA

Map of the Solent Area

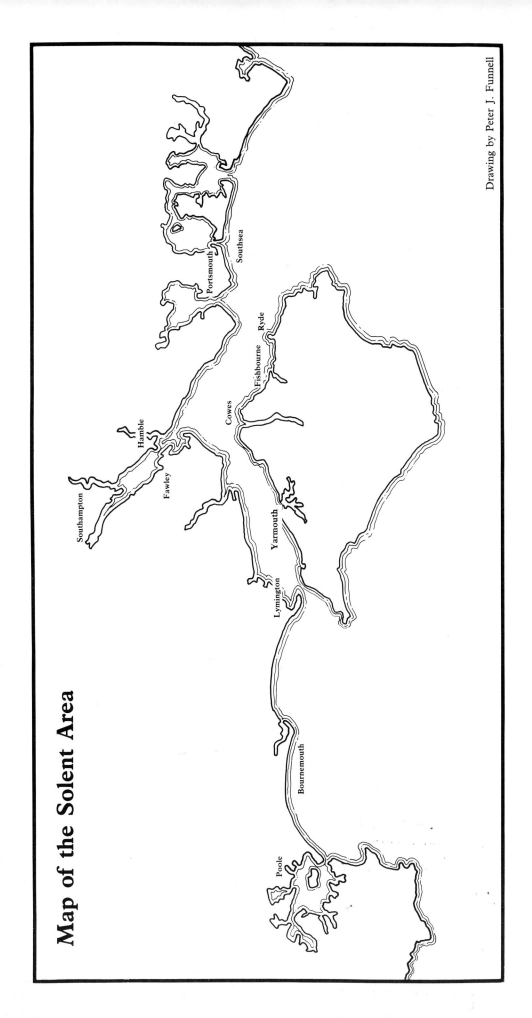

Southampton

Hamble

Fawley

Poole

Bournemouth

Lymington

Yarmouth

Cowes

Fishbourne Ryde

Portsmouth

Southsea

Drawing by Peter J. Funnell

Introduction

For centuries the Solent has been associated with maritime affairs; The Royal Navy perhaps making the largest presence at Portsmouth in earlier times. However, in Merchant Navy terms the Solent has been host to countless vessels, ranging from the great liners to hundreds of cargo ships, tankers, ferries and coasters. Perhaps with Southampton's double tides each day, the Solent has benefitted more than most other ports in attracting trade, plus of course its proximity to the Channel and the Atlantic.

This book is a review of the ships and other vessels using the Solent both at the present time and also those that used to grace the waters. Southampton is not alone today though in merchant marine activity — Portsmouth, Lymington and Poole too have their fair share of deep sea and local ferry operations and these are covered in some detail. Clearly changes in the actual ships visiting the Solent occur frequently but it is hoped that the tables included in the various sections portray a reasonably accurate survey of those seen regularly.

The foundation stone for Southampton Docks was laid on 12th October 1838 and so the 150th anniversary of that event will be celebrated during 1988. The first Dock was opened in 1842 but development was somewhat slow until the London & South Western Railway took over control in 1892. A major extension, consisting of what is now the Western Docks with a straight quay of 7,500 feet in length, was completed in the mid 1930s. Included in the work was the construction of the King George V drydock, which is still in use today and when completed was the largest drydock in the World.

For many years Southampton was the premier passenger port of the country, over 50% of all ocean going passengers arriving at or leaving the country from the port each year. In 1950 the Ocean Terminal was completed to cope with many of these passengers resulting in 1955 for instance in a total number of passengers using the port of 689,000. Indeed, even in 1969 a respectable 484,217 passengers passed through.

The Southern Railway and later British Railways operated cross channel services from Southampton for many years, and when these were withdrawn in the early 1960s their place was taken by various cross channel car ferries. The scene changed quickly, however, for space and facilities were made available at Portsmouth, resulting in the opening of the Continental Ferryport there in 1976. The Princess Alexandra Dock at Southampton, from where these ferries once operated, now forms part of the new Ocean Village complex.

By the late 1960s and early 1970s many of the passenger liners had gone and Southampton's trade changed radically. More and more shipping companies introduced containerisation and the need for special facilities to deal with these was soon obvious. This resulted in further land being reclaimed and the first berth to deal solely with container ships was brought into use in October 1968. Now containers are one of the most important factors in the economy of the port; during 1987 the equivalent of over 300,000 twenty foot container units passed through Southampton. The import and export of motor vehicles and the export of grain also now forms a major part of its trade.

Despite the great change the Solent has seen in the past decades in its variety of shipping movements, it can still boast one of the most interesting of waters and will continue to attract the attentions of enthusiastic onlookers and the all important customers.

Front cover; P&O Container's *Cardigan Bay*, well loaded with containers, sails past Dock Head at Southampton. A bulk carrier can be seen in the background loading grain. *Associated British Ports*

Back cover; Union Castle Line *Carnarvon Castle* (20,141 gross tons) at Southampton. She entered service in 1926 as a two funnelled ship being re-engined in 1937/8 for the new mail service to South Africa sporting just one funnel from that time. *Carnarvon Castle* was utilised as an Armed Merchant Cruiser and for trooping in World War Two and withdrawn from service completely in 1962. *The late D.T. Pye*

© Bert Moody &
Kingfisher Railway Productions
ISBN 0 946184 37 2
April 1988

Typeset by
Alphaset
65A The Avenue,
Southampton

Printed by
Riverside Printing Co.,
Reading,
Berks

Contents

Notes on the Details Given in the List of Ships

The details of the ships are shown under separate sections depending on the type of vessel, and each list is in alphabetical order. The year quoted is the year of completion of each ship, and is not necessarily the year the vessel was launched. Gross tonnage is not weight, but volume, as one gross ton equals 100 cubic feet of enclosed space. The length given in the tables is the overall length and this together with the breadth is given in metres. For those who still prefer to have this information in feet a conversion table is given below. The speed quoted is the normal service speed—one knot equals 1.151 miles per hour.

Conversion Table

1 metre = 3.3 feet	4 metres = 13.1 feet	50 metres = 164 feet
2 metres = 6.6 feet	5 metres = 16.4 feet	100 metres = 328 feet
3 metres = 9.8 feet	10 metres = 32.8 feet	

Passenger Liners & Cruise Ships

Nowadays the large passenger liners, which at one time were a major feature of the Solent area, are somewhat rare. Regular services by passenger ships are now practically a thing of the past, only Cunard's *Queen Elizabeth 2* still continues to make regular crossings of the North Atlantic, and even these are becoming less frequent. The emphasis today is on cruising, and in more recent years what has become known as 'Fly/Cruise' holidays have been developed with the result that the cruise ships do not return to their home ports, but are based in the Mediterranean or in American waters. Passengers are flown to and from the ship, so they can enjoy a longer period of cruising in warmer climates, and also avoid possible unpleasant voyages through the Bay of Biscay or across the Atlantic. The number of large passenger ships actually based on Southampton has been reduced to two — Cunard's *Queen Elizabeth 2* and P&O's *Canberra*.

The well known P&O cruise ship *Canberra*, built by Harland & Wolff Ltd. at Belfast. The *Canberra* made a name for herself during the Falklands conflict of 1982, being known by the troops as the 'Great White Whale'. *Bert Moody collection*

Name of Vessel	Built	Gross Tons	Overall Length metres	Breadth metres	Speed knots	Owners/Operators
Achille Lauro	1947	23,862	192	25	20	Lauro Line. (Italy)
Astor	1986	20,159	176	24	20	Astor Cruises (Mauritius)
Azerbaiydzhan	1975	13,252	156	22	21	USSR
Belorussiya	1975	13,251	156	22	21	USSR
Black Prince	1966	11,209	142	20	22	Fred Olsen, Norway (Philippines)
Canberra	1961	44,807	249	31	27	P&O SN Co Ltd.
Dmitriy Shostokovich	1980	9,878	134	21	19	USSR
Europa	1981	33,819	200	30	21	Hapag-Lloyd A.G. (Germany)
Gruziya	1975	13,252	156	22	21	USSR
Kazakhstan	1976	13,251	156	22	21	USSR
Maksim Gorkiy	1969	24,981	195	27	22	USSR
Neptune	1955	2,402	90	14	18	Epirotiki Lines (Greece)
Queen Elizabeth 2	1968	67,139	294	32	28½	Cunard Line Ltd.
Royal Viking Sea	1973	28,018	205	25	18	Royal Viking Line (Norwegian Cruise Lines)
Royal Viking Sky	1972	28,078	205	25	18	Royal Viking Line (Norwegian Cruise Lines)
Royal Viking Star	1972	28,221	205	25	18	Royal Viking Line (Norwegian Cruise Lines)
Sagafjord	1965	24,108	189	24	20	Cunard Line Ltd.
Vistafjord	1973	24,116	191	25	20	Cunard Line Ltd.

The Italian *Achille Lauro*, was completed in 1947 as Rotterdam Lloyd's *Willem Ruys* and as such called regularly while trading from Rotterdam to Indonesia. In 1959, after a major refit, the liner was placed on a round-the-world service from Rotterdam—Suez—Australia—New Zealand—Panama—Rotterdam. In 1964 she was sold to Lauro Lines and underwent a major refit during which her two funnels were replaced by the present aerodynamically shaped funnels. In October 1985 the liner was in the news, for while on a cruise in the Mediterranean armed Arab terrorists seized control of the ship for a time. *A. Duncan*

Queen Elizabeth 2—with her enlarged funnel fitted during a major refit carried out by Lloyd-Werft in Bremerhaven during the winter of 1986/7. During this refit her steam turbine machinery was replaced by diesel electric. The *Queen Elizabeth 2* was built by Upper Clyde Shipbuilders Ltd. on Clydebank.

F.R. Sherlock

Maksim Gorkily, easily recognised by her distinctive funnel, built as the German *Hamburg*, later renamed *Hanseatic*, before being acquired by the Russians in 1974 when she was given her present name. The liner is named after a Russian writer and politician who was born in 1868 and died in 1936.

F.R. Sherlock

Passenger & Car Ferries and Pleasure Vessels

The majority of the cross channel passenger/car ferries in the Solent area are now based on Portsmouth where special terminal facilities have been developed to handle the ever increasing traffic. Many more people now wish to take their cars with them when going on business or holiday to the Continent, and in addition there are regular movements of freight road vehicles to and from France. The demand for such accommodation at certain times of the year has resulted in larger and larger roll on/roll off ferries being constructed, while some of the existing vessels have been enlarged to carry more cars. P&O European Ferries (formerly Townsend Thoresen Ferries) operate services to Le Havre and Cherbourg, while Brittany Ferries serve Caen and St. Malo, and British Channel Islands Ferries operate to the Channel Islands. Sealink British Ferries run a summer service between Portsmouth, Cherbourg and the Channel Islands. Between Poole and Cherbourg Truckline Ferries operate a regular daily freight service, and during the summer months a passenger/car service in addition.

From Southampton the Red Funnel Group operate passenger/car ferries and hydrofoils to and from Cowes in the Isle of Wight, while Sealink British Ferries control the car ferries to and from the Isle of Wight from both Portsmouth and Lymington, and two high speed catamarans cover the Portsmouth—Ryde passenger service. There is also a hovercraft service between Southsea Beach and Ryde run by Hovertravel Ltd.

During the summer months there are a number of short cruises in the Solent operated by Sealink British Ferries and various smaller companies.

Above: Corbiere—built in 1970 as the Scandinavian ferry *Apollo*. She was the first of several similar vessels. Between 1976–1980 she was the *Olau Kent* operating between Sheerness and Vlissingen, and for the next four years was the *Gelting Nord*. In 1984 she became the *Benodet* operating on Brittany Ferries service between Plymouth and Roscoff being given her present name in 1985 and is now on the British Channel Islands Ferries service between Portsmouth and the Channel Islands.

Geoffrey Breeze

Left: Viking Viscount under overhaul in King George V drydock Southampton on 27th March 1988 and being repainted in the new P&O Ferries livery. This vessel operated out of Felixstowe until early 1986 when it was transferred to the Portsmouth operations. *Roger Hardingham*

Name of Vessel	Built	Gross Tons	Overall Length metres	Breadth metres	Speed knots	Owners/Operators
Armorique	1972	5,731	117	19	18½	Brittany Ferries
Bournemouth Belle	1975	50	26	9	10	Croson (Bournemouth)
Caedmon	1973	761	58	16	10	Sealink British Ferries
Cenred	1973	761	60	16	10	Sealink British Ferries
Cenwulf	1973	761	60	16	10	Sealink British Ferries
Corbiere	1970	4,371	109	17	17½	British Channel Islands Ferries
Cornouailles	1977	3,382	110	17	17	Brittany Ferries
Cowes Castle	1965	912	67	13	14	Red Funnel Group
Cuthred	1969	704	60	16	10	Sealink British Ferries
Darthula II	1939	46	17	8	8	M.G. Pearce
Duc De Normandie	1978	9,355	131	23	21	Brittany Ferries
Earl Granville	1973	4,657	109	17	19	Sealink British Ferries
Earl Harold	1971	3,909	113	17	19½	Sealink British Ferries
Gosport Queen	1966	159	30	9	9	Portsmouth Harbour Ferry Company
Gotland	1973	6,643	124	21	19	Brittany Ferries (Charter)
Hotspur IV	1946	54	19	6	9	Southern Coastcrafts Ltd. Hythe
Hythe Hotspur	1974	119	24	9	10	Southern Coastcrafts Ltd. Hythe
Island Enterprise	1974	46	25	8	9	Mursell, Kemp (Sandown)
Island Scene	1977	135	27	7	10	Blue Funnel Cruises
Leisure Scene	1985	150	31	7	10	Blue Funnel Cruises
Netley Castle	1974	1,183	74	15	14	Red Funnel Group
New Forester	1982	49	23	8	10	Southern Coastcrafts Ltd. Hythe
Norris Castle	1968	922	67	13	14	Red Funnel Group
Our Lady Pamela	1986	312	29	11	29½	Sealink British Ferries
Our Lady Patricia	1986	312	29	11	29½	Sealink British Ferries
Poole Belle	1977	49	28	9	10	Croson (Bournemouth)
Portelet	1967	3,987	110	18	19	British Channel Islands Ferries (charter)
Portsmouth Queen	1966	159	30	9	9	Portsmouth Harbour Ferry Company
Prince of Brittany	1970	5,465	119	18	18	Brittany Ferries
Solent Enterprise	1971	274	32	10	11	Portsmouth Harbour Ferry Company
Solent Scene	1974	131	27	7	10	Blue Funnel Cruises (W.C. Hogg and M.J. Rayment)
Southsea	1948	986	61	15	14	Sealink British Ferries
St. Catherine	1983	2,036	77	17	13	Sealink British Ferries
St. Cecilia	1987	2,970	79	17	13	Sealink British Ferries
St. Helen	1983	2,983	77	17	13	Sealink British Ferries
Viking Valiant	1975	14,760	137	22	21	P&O European Ferries Ltd.
Viking Venturer	1975	14,760	137	22	21	P&O European Ferries Ltd.
Viking Viscount	1976	6,387	129	20	21	P&O European Ferries Ltd.
Viking Voyager	1976	6,386	129	20	21	P&O European Ferries Ltd.

Earl Granville, flagship of Sealink British Ferries Channel Island service arrives at Portsmouth on 31st August 1987. This vessel has been on the Channel Island service since March 1981, being previously employed out of Stockholm as *Viking 4*.
Geoffrey Breeze

Name of Vessel	Built	Gross Tons	Overall Length metres	Breadth metres	Speed knots	Owners/Operators
Hydrofoils & Hovercraft						
Perservance (hovercraft)	1985	34	21	10	50	Hovertravel Ltd.
Shearwater 3 (hydrofoil)	1972	62	22	7	36½	Red Funnel Group
Shearwater 4 (hydrofoil)	1973	62	22	7	36½	Red Funnel Group
Shearwater 5 (hydrofoil)	1980	62	22	7	36½	Red Funnel Group
Shearwater 6 (hydrofoil)	1982	62	22	7	36½	Red Funnel Group
Tenacity (hovercraft)	1983	34	21	10	50	Hovertravel Ltd.

One of Red Funnel's fast hydrofoils, *Shearwater 6*, prepares to speed towards Cowes. This service began in 1969 and is now an accepted form of travelling to the Island. *Shearwater 6* was built in 1982 in Italy.

K.E. Adams

Norris Castle—one of the passenger/car ferries operated by the Red Funnel Group between Southampton and Cowes. When built by J.I. Thornycroft & Company at Woolston, the vessel was fitted for bow loading only, but was reconstructed in 1976 with stern loading doors, thus providing drive through facilities.

F.R. Sherlock

Cornouailles—this Norwegian built vessel has seen service on various routes operated by Brittany Ferries and in 1986 was utilised to provide a passenger/car ferry service from Poole to Cherbourg. This photograph shows her in Truckline Ferries livery while operating on that service. *R. Hardingham*

Centre left: St. Cecilia—one of three similar passenger/car ferries operated by Sealink British Ferries on the Portsmouth—Fishbourne (Isle of Wight) car ferry service. Accommodation available for 1,000 passengers and 142 cars.
Geoffrey Breeze

Centre right: Our Lady Patricia—during 1986 two high speed all welded aluminium constructed catamarans were introduced on Sealink's Portsmouth Harbour—Ryde passenger service to replace the conventional diesel ferries. Both catamarans were built by International Catamarans of Tasmania.
Sealink British Ferries

Right: Southsea—the last of the conventional diesel passenger ferries on the Portsmouth Harbour—Ryde service which were displaced by the high speed catamarans during 1986.
K.E. Adams

Ocean Going Container Ships

With the onset of containerisation the conventional cargo ship has practically disappeared, and when it is appreciated that one of these large container ships can carry the equivalent cargo on each voyage to that previously carried by four or five conventional cargo ships, it can be more easily understood as to why there are less ships to be seen in our waters. With containerisation many shipping companies have grouped together to provide joint services — in the case of Southampton the major operator trades under the name of Trio Lines — and operates between Europe and the Middle and Far East. Twenty container ships are regularly employed on these services controlled by British, German and Japanese companies — hence the title of Trio Lines. The companies involved are Ben Line Steamers Ltd., P&O Containers Ltd., Hapag-Lloyd A.G., Nippon Yusen Kaisha and Mitsui-OSK Lines K.K. In addition there is the service to and from South Africa, the main company being South African Marine Corporation, but other companies are involved. There is also a service to the Middle and Far East provided by the Norasia Group, which are now operating some of the most modern container ships afloat.

Frankfurt Express—one of the Hapag-Lloyd vessels in the Trio Lines operation. The ship has twin funnels and this can be seen in the photo above of the vessel being loaded at the Container berths at Southampton. One of the five large container cranes can be clearly seen together with one of the straddle carriers which are used to move the containers around the berths.

Above courtesy of Associated British Ports, below F.R. Sherlock

Name of Vessel	Built	Gross Tons	Overall Length metres	Breadth metres	Speed knots	Owners/Operators
Benalder	1972	55,889	289	32	22	Ben Line Steamers Ltd.
Benavon	1973	55,889	289	32	22	Ben Line Steamers Ltd.
Bremen Express	1972	57,366	287	32	23	Hapag-Lloyd A.G. (Germany)
Cardigan Bay	1972	56,822	290	32	23	P&O Containers Ltd.
City of Edinburgh	1973	55,889	289	32	22	Ben Line Steamers/Ellerman Lines
Frankfurt Express	1981	58,384	288	32	23	Hapag-Lloyd A.G. (Germany)
Hamburg Express	1972	58,087	288	32	23	Hapag-Lloyd A.G. (Germany)
Heemskerck	1978	51,982	259	32	23	Nedlloyd Lijnen B.V. (Netherlands)
Hongkong Express	1972	57,495	287	32	23	Hapag-Lloyd A.G. (Germany)
Kamakura Maru	1971	51,069	261	32	24	Nippon Yusen Kaisha (Japan)
Kasuga Maru	1976	58,440	289	32	25	Nippon Yusen Kaisha (Japan)
Kitano Maru	1972	51,269	261	32	24	Nippon Yusen Kaisha (Japan)
Kowloon Bay	1972	56,822	290	32	23	P&O Containers Ltd.
Kurama Maru	1972	59,407	290	32	23½	Nippon Yusen Kaisha (Japan)
Largs Bay	1977	52,007	259	32	23½	Nedlloyd Lijnen B.V. (P&O Containers Ltd.—charter)
Liverpool Bay	1972	56,822	290	32	23	P&O Containers Ltd.
Norasia Al Mansoorah	1987	21,633	187	28	17	Norasia Group—Arabian Maritime Line (F.Laeisz). (United Arab Emirates)
Norasia Al Muntazah	1987	23,760	201	28	17	Norasia Group—Arabian Maritime Line (United Arab Emirates)
Norasia Mubarak	1987	23,760	201	28	17	Norasia Group—Arabian Maritime Line (United Arab Emirates)
Norasia Pearl	1986	21,648	187	28	17	Norasia Group (F.Laeisz) (Germany)
Norasia Princess	1986	21,650	187	28	17	Norasia Group (F.Laeisz) (Germany)
Norasia Samantha	1985	19,527	173	28	17	Norasia Group (Germany)
Norasia Sharjah	1986	21,633	187	28	17	Norasia Group—Arabian Maritime Line (F.Laeisz) (United Arab Emirates)
Norasia Susan	1985	19,527	173	28	17	Norasia Group (Germany)
Osaka Bay	1973	56,822	290	32	23	P&O Containers Ltd.
Rhine Maru	1972	51,040	261	32	22	Mitsui-OSK Lines K.K. (Japan)
S.A. Helderberg	1977	52,615	258	32	20	South African Marine Corporation
S.A. Sederberg	1978	52,615	258	32	20	South African Marine Corporation
S.A. Waterberg	1979	52,615	258	32	20	South African Marine Corporation
S.A. Winterberg	1978	52,615	258	32	20	South African Marine Corporation
Thames Maru	1977	58,653	290	32	23	Mitsui-OSK Lines K.K. (Japan)
Tokio Express	1973	57,994	288	32	23	Hapag-Lloyd A.G. (Germany)
Tokyo Bay	1972	56,822	290	32	23	P&O Containers Ltd.

Kowloon Bay. One of five similar vessels operated by P&O Containers Ltd., each vessel capable of carrying the equivalent of 2,960 twenty foot containers.

F.R. Sherlock

Above: Benalder—well loaded with containers and operated by Ben Line Steamers on the Far East service of Trio Lines. *Benalder* was built in Germany by Howaldtswerke-Deutsche Werft at Kiel.

F.R. Sherlock

Centre: The *Kurama Maru*, one of the large container ships operated by Nippon Yusen Kaisha. When built in 1972 this vessel was fitted with steam turbines, but within the last few years, in order to effect an economy in fuel, the ship has been fitted with diesel engines, resulting in her speed being reduced by about three knots.

F.R. Sherlock

Bottom: S.A. Helderberg—one of four similar container ships owned by the South African Marine Corporation which operate between South Africa and Europe and the United Kingdom.

F.R. Sherlock

Bulk Carriers and Ocean Going Roll on/Roll Off Ships

Large bulk carriers can often be seen in the Solent area and the majority of them load grain from one of the two large grain terminals in the Eastern Docks at Southampton. Grain is now one of the more important commodities passing through the port—it is shipped to many parts of the world including Russia, Spain, Italy and Saudi Arabia. During the season ended July 1987 over 1.2 million tonnes of grain were exported through Southampton.

The following Roll on/Roll off vessels operate on a service to South Africa which was transferred from Tilbury to Southampton in 1987.

Name of Vessel	Built	Gross Tons	Overall Length metres	Breadth metres	Speed knots	Owners/Operators
Ango	1979	15,632	213	30	21½	SAECS (CGM/Chargeurs Reunis) (France)
CGM Ronsard	1980	15,632	213	30	21½	SAECS (CGM/Chargeurs Reunis) (France)
Kolsnaren	1978	21,722	217	32	20½	SAECS (Transatlantic Ship Management) (Sweden)

The Panamanian *Ugland Obo 5* (32,607 gross tons) built in 1984, a large bulk carrier loading grain from the Grain Terminal at 36 berth in Southampton Docks. Since this picture was taken several additional silos have been constructed on the site. *Associated British Ports*

Smaller Cargo and Container Vessels

A number of small feeder ships are involved in conveying containers to and from the Container berths at Southampton and various Continental and Irish ports. Commodore Shipping Company provide services from Portsmouth to the Channel Islands, and to Le Havre and Lisbon.

Various small cargo vessels can be seen regularly in the Solent, and normally these carry bulk cargoes such as grain, animal feed and fertiliser etc.

Name of Vessel	Built	Gross Tons	Overall Length metres	Breadth metres	Speed knots	Owners/Operators
Almirante	1970	1,971	100	14	14½	Fyffes Group (Honduras)
Barbara-Britt	1975	792	82	13	13½	Hans Schirren (Panama)
Carrigrennan	1970	377	45	9	10	Alderney Shipping Co. Ltd.
Clipper	1980	1,595	93	15	14	Moller Walther (Germany) (Scaniberia Line)
Commodore Clipper	1970	758	78	12	15½	Commodore Shipping Co.
Commodore Goodwill	1985	1,599	97	18	14	Commodore Shipping Co.
Confirmity	1979	499	56	9	11	F.T. Everard & Sons Ltd.
Elbe	1974	999	93	15	14	Bugsier Reederei und Bergungs A.G. (Germany)
El Mansour Stadi	1976	1,599	87	16	14	Soc. Marocaine de Nav. Maritime S.A. (Morocco)
Formality	1968	200	42	8	9	F.T. Everard & Sons Ltd.
Island Commodore	1971	589	79	11	12	Commodore Transport Ltd.
Mercandian Senator	1983	7,955	132	20	15½	Per Henriksen (K/s Merc-Scandia) (Denmark)
Murius	1962	125	30	6	9	Williams Shipping Co. (Fawley)
Nickerie	1985	4,233	108	18	16	Fyffes Group
Norman Commodore	1971	589	79	11	12	Commodore Transport Ltd.
Ocean Pride	1972	999	92	13	14	Gerd Koppelmann (Cyprus)
Oualidia	1978	1,593	96	14	14½	Comp. Marocaine de Nav. (Morocco)
Oulmes	1978	1,593	96	14	14½	Comp. Marocaine de Nav. (Morocco)
Owenglas	1970	729	78	12	12½	Contadora Panama S.A. (Panama) (MMD/Shipping Services)
Salrix	1965	656	65	10	10	J.R. Rix & Sons Ltd.
Sertan	1978	2,815	96	14	12½	Van Nievelt Goudriaan & Co. (Netherlands)
Siegerland	1974	778	77	13	13	Otto Albers J. Thode (Cyprus)
Singularity	1977	1,597	90	14	12½	F.T. Everard & Sons Ltd.
Triumph	1986	997	64	12	12	Beck's Scheepvaartkantoor B.V. (Netherlands)
Valiant	1977	1,599	80	14	12	Beck's Scheepvaartkantoor B.V. (Netherlands)
Vanda	1974	1,457	79	12	12	Beck's Scheepvaartkantoor B.V. (Netherlands)
Velox	1975	955	67	11	12	Beck's Scheepvaartkantoor B.V. (Netherlands)
Victress	1982	999	66	12	11	Beck's Scheepvaartkantoor B.V. (Netherlands)
Viscount	1976	955	66	11	12	Beck's Scheepvaartkantoor B.V. (Netherlands)
Walili	1980	2,075	91	16	15	Comp. de Transport Maritime S.A. (Morocco)

Singularity is owned by F.T. Everard & Sons who have a large fleet of over twenty-five coastal and short sea vessels, the majority of which end with the letters 'ITY'.

F.R. Sherlock

Above: Viscount—typical of many of the present day Dutch coasting vessels which are regular visitors to the Solent area.

Right: Commodore Clipper—one of the regular cargo vessels running between Portsmouth and the Channel Islands for Commodore Shipping Company.

F.R. Sherlock

Short Sea Car/Vehicle Carriers

Roll on/Roll off freight traffic is carried by the larger passenger/car ferries, but there are also smaller ones which cater only for freight traffic. Truckline Ferries run daily services for Roll on/Roll off freight traffic from Poole to Cherbourg. Many of the smaller car carriers can be regularly seen in the Solent area heading for Southampton with Renault cars from France or Fiats from Italy.

Name of Vessel	Built	Gross Tons	Overall Length metres	Breadth metres	Speed knots	Owners/Operators
Autoweg	1973	498	92	15	14	Ugland Bros. (UK)
Breizh-Izel	1970	2,769	112	17	17	Brittany Ferries/British Channel Island Ferries
Carbosco	1982	1,464	110	17	17	Interoll S.A. (Spain)
Castorp	1982	999	90	18	13	Lubeck Linie A.G. (Germany)
Cervantes	1984	4,198	141	22	14	Lineas Mar. Espanolas S.A. (Spain)
Coutances	1978	3,000	125	18	18	Truckline Ferries (France) S.A.
Donington	1976	1,591	106	16	15	Sirkit Sales Ltd. & C.W. Shipping Co. (St. Vincent)
Dora Baltea	1975	4,307	160	19	18	Grandi Traghetti S.p.A. (Italy)
Dora Riparia	1976	3,986	148	19	18	Atlantica S.p.A. Nav. (Italy)
Estoril	1974	1,592	100	16	15	Sirkit Sales & Walline Car Shipping Ltd. (St. Vincent)
Freccia Del Nord	1975	2,960	140	18	20	Grandi Traghetti S.p.A. (Italy)
Goodwood	1974	1,594	100	16	15	Sirkit Sales Ltd. & C.W. Shipping Co. (Isle of Man)
Hockenheim	1976	1,591	105	16	15	Sirkit Sales Ltd. & C.W. Shipping Co. (St. Vincent)
Le Castellet	1982	1,599	115	18	15	Soc. Francaise de Transportes Maritimes (France)
Po	1974	4,308	160	19	18½	Grimaldi Co. di Nav. & Siosa (Italy)
Purbeck	1978	3,000	125	18	18	Truckline Ferries (France) S.A.
Roline	1980	2,350	102	17	14	Roline S.A. (Spain)
Simbad	1981	1,464	109	16	15	Interoll S.A. (Bahamas)
Tiber	1970	2,163	96	19	15	Grimaldi Co. di Nav. & Siosa (Italy)

Freccia Del Nord. One of the Italian car carriers which are being used to bring in Fiats cars to the World Shipping Car Depot in Southampton Docks. The *Freccia Del Nord* is being assisted by Alexandra Towing Company's tug *Brockenhurst*, which no longer operates from Southampton.

F.R. Sherlock

Car & Vehicle Carriers

A major development in recent times has been the massive movement of new motor cars and vehicles around the world, and the ocean going car/vehicle carriers still continue to get larger—in effect they are large floating garages and some of them can accommodate over 6,000 cars. So far as Southampton is concerned the larger carriers are mainly involved with the export of cars and vehicles to America and the Middle and Far East.

Name of Vessel	Built	Gross Tons	Overall Length metres	Breadth metres	Speed knots	Owners/Operators
Carmen	1982	18,661	200	33	18	Walleniusrederierna. (Sweden)
Clover Ace	1982	17,417	199	30	18	Mitsui OSK & Shinyei Sen. K.K. (Japan))
Don Juan	1975	14,480	203	28	19	Walleniusrederierna (Singapore)
Falstaff	1985	51,858	202	32	19½	Walleniusrederierna (Sweden)
Faust	1985	51,858	202	32	19½	Walleniusrederierna (Sweden)
Figaro	1981	18,661	200	33	19½	Walleniusrederierna (Sweden)
Glorious Ace	1981	16,880	190	33	19	Mitsui OSK & Bala Daiko Shosen K.K. (Japan)
Isolde	1985	51,071	200	32	19½	Walleniusrederierna (Sweden)
Madame Butterfly	1981	18,728	200	32	19½	Walleniusrederierna (Sweden)
Medea	1982	18,661	200	32	19½	Walleniusrederierna (Sweden)
Oberon	1974	12,139	197	28	19	Wallenius (Singapore)
Pacific Breeze	1986	21,237	196	29	19	Wallenius Line & Fuji Shipping Co. (Japan)
Rigoletto	1977	17,502	190	32	19	Walleniusrederierna (Sweden)
Tosca	1978	16,883	196	32	19	Walleniusrederierna (Sweden)
Traviata	1977	17,511	190	32	19	Walleniusrederierna (Sweden)
Tristan	1985	51,071	200	32	19½	Walleniusrederierna (Sweden)

Above: Isolde. One of the vessels in the Wallenius fleet—the *Isolde* is loading a consignment of Jaguar cars at Southampton for America. This ship can carry over 6,000 cars.
Associated British Ports

Right: Medea. All the car/vehicle carriers operated by the Swedish Company of Wallenius are named after well known characters in operas. Each of these vessels can accommodate up to 5,000 cars.
F.R. Sherlock

Tankers

Large tankers can be seen regularly in the Solent bringing in crude oil to the Esso Refinery at Fawley, located on the west side of Southampton Water. Some of this oil originates from the offshore installations in the North Sea. The refinery at Fawley handles over 20 million tonnes of all grades of petroleum oil each year. In 1986, 2,800 tankers of all sizes called at the Refinery jetties, which consist of five ocean berths and four coastal berths.

Smaller tankers, including many liquified gas carriers, distribute the refined products to the Continent and around the coast of Britain.

At Hamble, on the east side of Southampton Water, BP Oil Ltd. have a jetty serving their depot which is used for distribution and storage, and this is normally served by coastwise shipping.

Above: Esso Demetia—has operated between Sullom Voe and the Esso Refinery at Fawley bringing in oil from the North Sea oilfields. *F.R. Sherlock*

Left: Berkeley a coastal tanker operated by Bowker & King Ltd. *F.R. Sherlock*

Name of Vessel	Built	Gross Tons	Overall Length metres	Breadth metres	Speed knots	Owners/Operators
Drupa	1966	39,796	244	34	14	Shell Tankers (UK) Ltd.
Esso Aberdeen	1967	58,273	277	42	17	Esso Petroleum Co.
Esso Africa	1975	137,166	349	52	15	Esso Tankers Inc. (Liberia)
Esso Albany	1973	12,805	161	24	15	Esso Petroleum Co.
Esso Bermuda	1974	126,192	348	52	15	Esso International Shipping (Bahamas)
Esso Clyde	1972	12,317	166	23	15½	Esso Petroleum Co.
Esso Demetia	1973	125,293	341	52	16	Esso Petroleum Co.
Esso Fawley	1967	11,064	163	22	16½	Esso Petroleum Co.
Esso Mersey	1972	12,323	166	23	15	Esso Petroleum Co.
Esso Milford Haven	1967	10,902	163	22	16½	Esso Petroleum Co.
Esso Severn	1975	12,316	166	23	15½	Esso Petroleum Co.
Esso Tees	1970	12,683	170	24	17	Esso Petroleum Co.
Esso Warwickshire	1962	48,049	263	34	17	Esso Petroleum Co.
Northia	1971	68,286	280	41	15½	Shell Tankers (UK) Ltd.

Short Sea Tankers

Name of Vessel	Built	Gross Tons	Overall Length metres	Breadth metres	Speed knots	Owners/Operators
Activity	1969	698	74	10	12	F.T. Everard & Sons Ltd.
Allurity	1969	698	74	10	12	F.T. Everard & Sons Ltd.
Ann Lise Tholstrup★	1963	500	52	9	10	Kosan Tankers A/S (Denmark)
Asperity	1967	698	74	10	12	F.T. Everard & Sons Ltd.
Barrier	1958	487	52	10	9	Bowker & King Ltd.
Beckenham	1980	825	64	12	11	Bowker & King Ltd.
Beckton	1971	239	40	7	8	Bowker & King Ltd.
Bencleuch	1976	1,599	81	13	13½	Ben Line Steamers Ltd.
Benmacdhui	1976	1,596	81	13	13½	Ben Line Steamers Ltd.
Berkeley	1969	730	65	9	10	Bowker & King Ltd.
Betina Tholstrup★	1969	3,061	102	14	13	Kosan Tankers A/S (Singapore)
Birtha Tholstrup★	1962	1,044	63	9	13½	Kosan Tankers A/S (Denmark)
Blackheath	1980	751	60	11	11	Bowker & King Ltd.
Borkum	1970	1,242	93	13	12	Leth & Co. (Germany)
B.P. Hunter	1980	1,595	82	15	14	BP Oil Ltd.
B.P. Jouster	1972	1,598	79	13	12	BP Oil Ltd.
B.P. Warrior	1968	1,529	76	12	12	BP Oil Ltd.
Brentwood	1980	994	70	11	11	Bowker & King Ltd.
Cableman	1980	4,916	117	17	13	Rowbotham Tankships Ltd.
Esso Avon	1981	1,599	91	13	12	Esso Petroleum Co.
Esso Penzance	1971	2,178	91	13	13	Esso Petroleum Co.
Esso Plymouth	1980	1,421	71	13	11½	Esso Petroleum Co.
Esso Tenby	1970	2,170	91	13	13	Esso Petroleum Co.
Eva Tholstrup★	1958	499	65	10	11½	Kosan Tankers A/S (Denmark)
Happy Bird★	1968	1,231	68	12	12½	Naess Shipping (Philippines)
Happy Fellow★	1967	1,334	71	12	12½	Naess Shipping (Philippines)
Knud Tholstrup★	1982	1,999	77	14	12	Kosan Tankers A/S (Denmark)
Lisbet Tholstrup★	1963	1,367	85	10	12	Kosan Tankers A/S (Singapore)
Mare Altum	1974	1,597	81	14	13½	Nedlloyd Bulkchem (Netherlands)
Ninja Tholstrup★	1964	500	52	9	10	Kosan Tankers A/S (Denmark)
Oilman	1962	997	65	11	11	Rowbotham Tankships Ltd.
Olav Trygvason★	1975	3,959	102	17	14	Olav Trygvason (Liberia)
Prins Philips Willem★	1985	1,552	64	14	11½	A.Veder & Co. B.V. (Netherlands)
Prins Willem II★	1985	1,552	64	14	11½	A.Veder & Co. B.V. (Netherlands)
Shell Craftsman	1968	1,529	76	12	14	Shell (UK) Ltd.
Shell Engineer	1966	1,177	66	11	11	Shell (UK) Ltd.
Shell Marketer	1981	1,599	79	13	12	Shell (UK) Ltd.
Shell Seafarer	1981	1,599	79	13	12	Shell (UK) Ltd.
Shell Supplier	1972	1,210	66	11	11	Shell (UK) Ltd.
Shell Technician	1982	1,599	79	13	12	Shell (UK) Ltd.
Shell Trader	1966	1,177	66	11	11	Shell (UK) Ltd.
Tine Tholstrup★	1967	1,395	71	12	12	Kosan Tankers A/S (Singapore)

★liquified gas carrier.

Cableman—owned by Rowbotham Tankships and has called at BP Hamble Jetty. As the tanker is empty she is riding high in the water and part of her bulbous bow can be seen.   *F.R. Sherlock*

Shell Marketer one of the more modern coastal tankers owned by Shell (UK) Ltd.   *F.R. Sherlock*

Tugs

Wherever large ships are involved one will find tugs, although nowadays with the introduction of bow and stern side thrust propellers the need for tugs is not so great as it was. At Southampton two companies share all the main work—Alexandra Towing Company and the Red Funnel Group. The latter company also have two fire fighting tugs—the *Gatcombe* and *Vecta* based off the Esso Refinery at Fawley.

Name of Vessel	Built	Gross Tons	Overall Length metres	Breadth metres	Speed knots	Owners/Operators
Accomplice	1944	80	22	5	10	Husbands Shipyards, Marchwood
Adherence	1944	54	20	5	9	Husbands Shipyards, Marchwood
Albert	1972	272	33	9	12	Alexandra Towing Company
Assurance	1944	65	20	5	9	Husbands Shipyards, Marchwood
Clausentum	1980	334	33	10	12	Red Funnel Group
Flying Kestrel	1976	223	29	9	11	Alexandra Towing Company
Flying Osprey	1976	223	29	9	11	Alexandra Towing Company
Gatcombe	1970	269	33	9	12½	Red Funnel Group
Hamtun	1985	250	29	9	10	Red Funnel Group
MST Lock	1944	76	19	6	8	Marine Support & Towage (Cowes)
Presstan	1950	67	21	6	8	Marine Support & Towage (Cowes)
Sir Bevois	1985	250	29	9	10	Red Funnel Group
Sun XXIV	1962	113	27	7	12	Alexandra Towing Company
Totland	1961	208	29	7	10	Red Funnel Group
Vecta	1970	269	33	9	12½	Red Funnel Group
Ventnor	1965	173	31	8	12	Alexandra Towing Company
Wyepull	1985	50	20	5	9	Itchen Marine Towage Ltd.

Gatcombe—one of two fire fighting tugs of the Red Funnel Group normally based off the Esso Refinery at Fawley. Built by R. Dunston Ltd. at Hessle.   *F.R. Sherlock*

Hamtun—one of three tractor type tugs in use by Red Funnel Group. Two of these tugs, of which *Hamtun* is one, were built specially for the Group, and are fitted with twin screw Schottel azimuthing propeller units which provides for much improved manoeuvrability and enables the tug to tow sideways as well as forward and aft.

F.R. Sherlock

Brittany Ferries *Armorique*, completed in Le Havre in 1972 as the *Terje Vigen* for J.S. Hagen of Norway, and designed for the Aarhus—Oslo service. Shortly afterwards she was sold to Skan Fahre K.G. of Germany from whom Brittany Ferries acquired the vessel in 1975, entering Brittany Ferries service in March 1976 operating between Plymouth and Roscoff. She was later transferred to the Portsmouth—St. Malo service providing accommodation for 700 passengers and 180 cars. At times the *Armorique* has been used as a relief ship and has served on all the Brittany Ferries routes.

Geoffrey Breeze

Petimata OT RMS (23,104 gross tons) a Bulgarian bulk carrier loading grain at 47 berth in the Ocean Dock. This vessel is typical of the type of bulk carriers which can regularly be seen loading grain in Southampton.

M. Beckett

The P&O *Iberia* (29,779 gross tons) built by Harland & Wolff of Belfast laid-up in Southampton on 20th May 1972. This vessel was used on the London—Australia service until later years when it concentrated on cruising, calling frequently at Southampton.   *Bert Moody*

An impressive view of the King George V drydock in Southampton showing the *Queen Mary* under repair. Note the large number of Renault cars and the area to the top right which is now reclaimed and forms the Container Terminal.   *Bert Moody collection*

Assurance one of the smaller tugs to be seen in the area. Owned by Husbands Shipyards at Marchwood, she was originally one of the standard 'TID' wartime built tugs. Rebuilt by Husbands Shipyards in 1965 and fitted with a diesel engine. *F.R. Sherlock*

Flying Osprey—one of two similar tugs operated by Alexandra Towing Company at Southampton. Formerly the German *Cornelie Wessels*, she is fitted with Schottel azimuthing propellers and was acquired by the Company in 1986. *F.R. Sherlock*

Dredger/Aggregate carriers

For many years now there has been in the Solent area a considerable traffic in seaborne aggregate. This is dredged by suction from the sea bed at certain specified areas off the Isle of Wight and the mainland. Some of the vessels used have been specially built for the purpose, while others have been converted from coastal tankers or cargo vessels.

Name of Vessel	Built	Gross Tons	Overall Length metres	Breadth metres	Speed knots	Owners/Operators
Afan	1961	918	61	12	10	Northwood (Fareham) Ltd.
Arco Scheldt	1972	1,583	77	14	12	ARC Marine Ltd.
Arco Severn	1974	1,599	81	14	12	ARC Marine Ltd.
Arco Test	1971	594	64	10	10	ARC Marine Ltd.
Arco Tyne	1975	2,684	98	15	13	ARC Marine Ltd.
Glen Gower	1963	552	52	9	10	Northwood (Fareham) Ltd.
Hexhamshire Lass	1955	561	48	10	10	Cortend Ltd.—Northwood (Fareham) Ltd.
KB	1948	299	42	7	8	Kendall Bros (Portsmouth) Ltd.
KB II	1960	552	52	9	10	Kendall Bros (Portsmouth) Ltd.
Sand Gull	1964	534	53	9	9	South Coast Shipping Co.
Sand Lark	1963	540	53	9	9	South Coast Shipping Co.
Sand Robin	1950	116	28	6	7	Bedhampton Sand & Gravel Co.
Sand Swan	1970	1,164	66	12	10	South Coast Shipping Co.
Sand Swift	1969	1,162	66	12	10	South Coast Shipping Co.
Sand Tern	1963	535	53	9	9	South Coast Shipping Co.
Solent Lee	1959	756	62	9	10	Northwood (Fareham) Ltd.
Steel Welder	1955	500	52	9	9	Northwood (Fareham) Ltd.

Sand Swift was built specially as a suction dredge/aggregate carrier for South Coast Shipping. This view shows the vessel coming up the River Itchen fully loaded. The hold is 22 metres in length and can contain about 1,000 tons. *F.R. Sherlock*

Above: Hexhamshire Lass heading out to sea from the River Itchen to dredge another cargo of aggregate. The end of the dredge pipe can be seen being held by the small derrick. This vessel was built as a hopper barge for the Central Electricity Authority to convey fly ash for dumping at sea from power stations on the Tyne. She was converted to a suction dredger in 1972.

F.R. Sherlock

Left: S.H.B. Seahorse—a buoy tender built for Southampton Harbour Board and in 1968 transferred to British Transport Docks Board when that authority took over the responsibilities of the Southampton Harbour Board.

F.R. Sherlock

Miscellaneous Ships

There are various other interesting types of ships which can be seen—one such type is the cable ship; British Telecom International have a depot in the Western Docks at Southampton, while Standard Telephone & Cable Company have a cable factory on the Western Docks estate. Also on the Dock estate is a large bottling factory for Martini, the wine arriving in special wine tankers and pumped ashore to the factory. There is also Rank's Mill which is served by various coasters bringing in grain. The Corporation of Trinity House operates several lighthouse tenders and one often seen in the Solent is the *Stella*.

Of the preserved ships the paddle steamer *Waverley* and the motor vessel *Balmoral* are both fully operational. The *Waverley* usually spends two weeks in the Solent during September of each year. The *Galway Bay* which was originally the Red Funnel Group's tug/tender *Calshot* and the sludge carrier *Shieldhall* will, it is hoped, form part of the Maritime Museum complex based on the Ocean Village at Southampton. The *Shieldhall* is of special interest for she is fitted with triple expansion engines and is still a steam vessel.

Name of Vessel	Built	Gross Tons	Overall Length metres	Breadth metres	Speed knots	Type of vessel	Owners/Operators
Cable Venture	1962	9,019	152	19	12½	cable ship	Cable & Wireless Plc.
C.S. Alert	1961	6,083	127	17	14	cable ship	British Telecom International
C.S. Iris	1976	3,874	97	15	15	cable ship	British Telecom International
C.S. Monarch	1975	3,874	97	15	15	cable ship	British Telecom International
Greendale H	1962	311	43	7	7½	sludge vessel	Effluents Services Ltd.
Mancunium	1946	1,378	80	12	10	sludge vessel	Effluents Services Ltd.
Mercury	1962	8,862	144	18	16	cable ship	Cable & Wireless Plc. (Bermuda)
Mermaid	1987	2,820	80	15	12	lighthouse/buoy tender	Corporation of Trinity House
Northam Osprey	1982	115	28	7	9	pollution control vessel	BP International Ltd.
Odet	1975	1,599	90	14	13	wine tanker	N.T. Vinicoles Leduc S.A. (France)
Pic Saint Loup	1974	1,599	89	14	13	wine tanker	N.T. Vinicoles Leduc S.A. (France)
Pointe de Lesven	1975	1,599	91	13	13	wine tanker	S.F.C. (France)
Rhone	1974	1,599	90	14	13	wine tanker	Vinalmar S.A. (Switzerland)
SHB Seahorse	1958	156	27	8	8	buoy tender	Associated British Ports
Stella	1961	1,425	67	12	13	lighthouse tender	Corporation of Trinity House
Swansea Bay	1966	2,941	94	16	12	suction dredger	Associated British Ports
Preserved Ships							
Balmoral	1949	688	62	10	14	pleasure vessel	Waverley Excursions Ltd.
Galway Bay (to be renamed Calshot)	1930	702	45	10	13	tug/tender	Southampton City Council
Shieldhall	1955	1,752	82	14	13	sludge carrier	Southern Water Authority
Waverley	1947	693	73	17	14	paddle steamer	Waverley Excursions Ltd.
Sail Training Ships							
Lord Nelson	1986	400	43	8	—		Jubilee Sailing Trust
Malcolm Miller	1967	219	41	7	—		Sail Training Association
Royalist	1971	83	23	6	—		Sea Cadet Association
Sir Winston Churchill	1966	219	41	7	—		Sail Training Association

Rhone—a bulk wine carrier flying the Swiss flag. The wine is pumped ashore from the tanker direct to the Martini Bottling factory on the Western Dock Estate at Southampton. During 1986 thirty million litres of Martini were received for bottling and distribution throughout the United Kingdom.

F.R. Sherlock

Above: Stella—one of the Trinity House's lighthouse tenders which can be regularly seen in the Solent. These ships are also engaged in the maintenance and replacement of navigational buoys. *F.R. Sherlock*

Left: C.S. Iris—one of two similar ships built by Robb-Caledon at Dundee in 1976. The other one is *C.S. Monarch*. They are both owned by Midland Montague Leasing Ltd. and are on charter to British Telecom International. The two vessels operate from the British Telecom International Marine Depot at 203 berth, which was opened in 1974. Each vessel has ten cable tanks—four main tanks on the centre line and three smaller tanks on each side. *C.S. Iris* was requisitioned for the Falkland Islands operations in 1982. *F.R. Sherlock*

Shieldhall—a sludge carrier which is at present being preserved in Southampton. The vessel, which originally operated on the River Clyde, was acquired by the Southern Water Authority in 1977 and was finally withdrawn from service in July 1985. The *Shieldhall* is one of the few ships still afloat with steam triple expansion engines, and can be seen in the Ocean Village complex at Southampton.   *F.R. Sherlock*

Above: Balmoral—formerly a vessel of the Red Funnel fleet at Southampton, but now operated by Waverley Excursions at various locations around the coast of Britain.   *K.E. Adams*

Right: Waverley—completed in 1947 for the London & North Eastern Railway for service on the Clyde. She subsequently came under the control of Caledonian MacBrayne Ltd. and was withdrawn from service in 1973, and then acquired by the Paddle Steamer Preservation Society. The *Waverley* is now operated by Waverley Excursions, and usually visits the Solent area for two weeks during September of each year. *K.E. Adams*

Ships of the Past in Solent Waters

What better way to start this section of the book than with the two Cunard *Queens*, together at Southampton on 25th January 1962—the *Queen Mary* (81,237 gross tons) having sailed from the Western Docks for New York, while the *Queen Elizabeth* (83,673 gross tons) is about to leave her berth at the Ocean Terminal in the Ocean Dock to move to King George V drydock for her annual overhaul.

The *Queen Mary*, which was completed in 1936 by John Brown & Company Ltd. on Clydebank, left Southampton for the last time on 31st October 1967, and is now a Hotel and Conference centre at Long Beach, California. The *Queen Elizabeth* completed by the same builder in 1940, was destroyed by fire in January 1972 in Hong Kong harbour while being fitted out to become a floating university.

Southern Newspapers

Cunard's *Queen Elizabeth* at the Ocean Terminal in the Ocean Dock at Southampton. The Terminal was officially opened on 31st July 1950 by the then Prime Minister, the Rt. Hon. C.R. Atlee, and it was used for the first time on the following day when passengers embarked on to the *Queen Elizabeth* sailing to New York. The building was demolished in June 1983, and the area is now used for the storage and loading of scrap metal.

Bert Moody collection

ARUNDEL CASTLE.

One of the Union Castle Company's four funnellers—the *Arundel Castle* was completed in 1921 by Harland & Wolff Ltd. at Belfast. The other four funneller in the Company's fleet was the *Windsor Castle*, which was sunk during the war. In 1936 the Union Castle Company signed a new agreement with the South African Government in respect of the mail contract and it was necessary to accelerate the service to meet the requirements of this new contract resulting in several vessels in the fleet being re-engined. The *Arundel Castle* returned to her builders in 1937 for this work to be carried out, and the opportunity was taken to modernise the vessel, returning to service with only two funnels and a curved bow. In 1940 she was converted to a troop transport and before being released from Government service in 1949 had steamed a total of 564,000 miles. She was then refitted and re-entered the mail service in September 1950—her gross tonnage was then 19,216 and accommodation was provided for 168 first and 371 tourist class passengers. The *Arundel Castle* left Southampton for the last time in December 1958 and was broken up in Hong Kong during 1959.

Bert Moody collection

The troopship *Dilwara*, (12,555 gross tons), completed in 1935 by Barclay Curle on the Clyde, she was the first purpose-built troop transport of this century, all the previous troopships being converted from merchant ships. Southampton was the home of peacetime trooping from 1894 until 1962 when the last of the troopships was withdrawn from service, all peacetime commitments then being covered by aircraft. Pre-war the *Dilwara* was one of the first troopships to carry out educational voyages to Scandinavian countries during the off-trooping season. During the war the vessel saw service in many theatres of operations. In 1949/50 the *Dilwara* was completely refitted and her accommodation reduced to 329 cabin berths and 705 bunks in Standee three tiers. She was withdrawn from trooping service in 1960 and was then acquired by the China Navigation Company and was renamed *Kuala Lumpur*, being used as a pilgrim ship until 1971 when she was broken up in Taiwan. *Bert Moody collection*

Opposite page top: *Aquitania* (45,647 gross tons) the last of the real four funnellers, completed by John Brown & Company on Clydebank in 1914 for the Cunard Steamship Company. She made her maiden voyage from Liverpool to New York on 30th May of that year, but after only three round trips the war broke out, and the liner was taken up for war service. Initially she was to be used as an armed merchant cruiser, but she became a hospital ship and later a troop transport vessel. Cunard transferred their express service from Liverpool to Southampton in 1919 and from then onwards the *Aquitania* could be regularly seen in Solent waters.

Never a record breaker, the *Aquitania* established herself as a very popular and comfortable ship in which to travel. She operated regularly on the North Atlantic route with such ships as the *Berengaria* and the *Mauretania*, and later with the *Queen Mary*. During the Second World War the liner was used as a troopship, carrying 384,580 passengers and steaming 526,260 miles on war service. At the end of the war she made several voyages from this country to Canada with Canadian war brides and their children.

The *Aquitania* was released from war service in March 1948 although arrangements had been made with the Canadian Government for the liner to make a series of voyages between Southampton and Halifax mainly with immigrants. These voyages were completed when the *Aquitania* arrived in Southampton on 1st December 1949. She was then laid up until sold for scrap, leaving the port for the last time on 19th February 1950 for Faslane, where she was broken up. *Bert Moody collection*

Opposite page bottom: *Empress of Britain* (42,348 gross tons), completed in 1931 by John Brown & Company on Clydebank for Canadian Pacific Steamships. The liner was built for two purposes—first the summer North Atlantic service from Southampton to Quebec on the St. Lawrence River, and secondly for world-wide cruising during the winter months when the River St. Lawrence was closed to shipping. From 1931 until 1938 each winter the *Empress of Britain* made a world-wide cruise from Southampton, usually leaving at the end of November and returning during the following April. On the outbreak of war the *Empress of Britain* was refitted for use as a troop transport, and became the largest merchant ship lost by the Allies during the war, being sunk on 28th October 1940 by torpedoes after being set on fire by a German long range bomber some 70 miles north-west of Ireland. *Bert Moody collection*

Two of P&O's cruise ships—the *Orsova* (28,790 gross tons) and the *Chusan* (24,062 gross tons) in the Western Docks at Southampton in 1968. Both vessels were regular visitors to the port during the 1950s and 1960s.

The *Orsova* was built for the Orient Line by Vickers-Armstrongs at Barrow, being completed in 1954, making her first appearance at Southampton on 9th July of that year at the end of a Mediterranean cruise. The liner was one of the first large ships to dispense entirely with conventional masts. In 1960 the Orient Line was merged with P&O SN Company. The *Orsova* was broken up in Taiwan during 1974.

The *Chusan* was built for P&O's Far Eastern service, being completed in 1950 by Vickers Armstrongs at Barrow. She made her maiden voyage on 1st July 1950 sailing from Southampton on an eight day cruise to Madeira and Lisbon. The special fitting which can be seen at the top of the funnel on the *Chusan* was designed by J.I. Thornycroft & Company Ltd. at Woolston to lift smoke, smuts and fumes off the decks of the ship. The *Chusan* was scrapped in Taiwan

Bert Moody collection

Right/Below: P&O Strathnaver (22,547 gross tons) built in 1931 by Vickers Armstrong at Barrow in Furness and operated mainly in the London—Australia service, but during the summer months the liner made occasional cruises from Southampton. The vessel was fitted with turbo-electric machinery the first and third funnels being dummies. Befitted for commercial work in 1949, she returned to P&O service with only one funnel. The liner was broken up at Hong Kong in 1962.

Bert Moody collection

Right: The *Strathmore* (23,500 gross tons) was completed in 1935 for P&O SN Co., being launched from Vickers Armstrong's yard at Barrow in Furness by the then Duchess of York (now Queen Elizabeth the Queen Mother). During the war the *Strathmore* served as a troopship taking part in the North African landings. In 1963 the vessel was sold to the Greek firm of John Latsis, being first renamed *Marianna Latsi*, and later *Henrietta Latsi*, being broken at La Spezia in 1969.

Bert Moody collection

These photographs show two of the [...]
phases in the life of the Royal Mail Li[...]
Andes (25,676 gross tons) which [...]
completed by Harland & Wolff [...]
Belfast in 1939, and was due to mak[...]
maiden voyage from Southamtpo[...]
South America in September of that [...]
However the war intervened and the [...]
was used as a troopship. One of [...]
notable voyages was in May 1945 whe[...]
carried the Norweigian Government [...]
to Oslo after exile. The *Andes* was re[...]
as a passenger liner in 1947 [...]
accommodation for 530 passengers [...]
made her first commercial voyage [...]
Southampton to South America on [...]
January 1948 (pictured above).

By the end of the 1950s with [...]
considerable advance of air travel th[...]
of such a large passenger ship on the [...]
American service could no longe[...]
justified and during the early part of [...]
Andes was fitted out as a cruise [...]
(picture left) by 'De Schelde' at Vliss[...]
with accommodation for 470 passen[...]
Early in 1971 she was sold for scra[...]
was broken up by van Heyghen Fre[...]
Ghent. *Bert Moody coll[...]

Northern Star (24,756 gross tons) was designed to operate on a round the world service with the *Southern Cross* for Shaw, Savill & Albion. She was launched by Queen Elizabeth, the Queen Mother, on 27th June 1961 from Vickers-Armstrongs' yard at Walker-on-Tyne, and sailed on her maiden voyage to Australia and New Zealand from Southampton on 10th July 1962. *Northern Star* was a fully air-conditioned vessel with accommodation for 1,420 passengers. She had a rather short life for she was sold for scrap at the end of 1974 being broken up at Kaohsiung, Taiwan. Somewhat surprisingly her sister ship, the *Southern Cross* built seven years earlier, is still afloat today, renamed the *Azure Seas* and is cruising mainly off the Pacific Coast of America.

Nieuw Amsterdam (36,982 gross tons), of the Holland American Line, a most popular ship for many years. She was launched on 10th April 1937 by Queen Wilhelmina and called at Southampton for the first time on 10th May 1938 when on her maiden voyage from Rotterdam to New York. After a major refit after the war she returned to the North Atlantic service in October 1947, and continued to operate on that service until the late 1960s after which she was used entirely for cruising. After 36 years she was broken up in Taiwan. *Bert Moody collection*

The *Rotterdam* (38,645 gross tons), a very popular ship, was completed in 1959 for the Holland America Line for their Rotterdam—Southampton—New York service on which the liner operated for nearly ten years. Accommodation was provided for 1,400 passengers in two classes. From 1969 the *Rotterdam* has been employed entirely on cruising, mainly from American ports. The vessel is now operated by Holland America Cruises Inc., and has accommodation for 1,000 passengers.   *F.R. Sherlock*

The steamship *Statendam* (24,294 gross tons) was completed at the end of 1956 for the Holland America Line, and made her first call at Southampton on her maiden voyage to New York on 8th February 1957. From 1966 the vessel was used entirely for cruising.
In 1982 the *Statendam* was sold and renamed *Rhapsody*, and in 1987 her steam turbines were replaced by diesel engines, renamed *Regent Star*, and is now cruising in the Caribbean.   *F.R. Sherlock*

The *Bremen* (32,336 gross tons), the fifth North German Lloyd liner to bear the name, called at Southampton for the first time on 10th July 1959 after which she became a regular caller for the next ten years.

The ship was completed in 1939 by Chantier et Ateliers de St. Nazaire Penhoet for Compangie de Navigation Sud-Atlantique as the *Pasteur* and was scheduled to make her maiden voyage in September 1939, but owing to the outbreak of war this was cancelled.

She was eventually used as a troopship under Cunard management and at the end of hostilities in Europe the *Pasteur* made several appearances at Southampton. In 1946 she was handed back to the French who used her to take troops to Indo-China until the end of 1956, after which she was laid up at Brest. In July 1957 she was acquired by North German Lloyd and completely refitted as a passenger ship by Bremer Vulkan. In 1972 she was taken over by the Chandris Group and renamed *Regina Magna*, and in 1977 became an accommodation ship at Jeddah, under the name of *Saudi-Filipinas* and in 1980 was sold for scrap. While being towed to Taiwan she sank in the Arabian Sea on the 9th June of that year.

The *Isle of Jersey*, one of the three well known 'Isles' owned and operated by the Southern Railway and later British Railways on their Southampton—Channel Islands services. The other two vessels were the *Isle of Guernsey* and the *Isle of Sark*. All three were built by William Denny & Brothers Ltd. of Dumbarton, with the *Isle of Jersey* being completed in 1930. During the war she was fitted out as a hospital ship and made a number of trips with wounded in 1944 from the Normandy Beaches to Southampton.
Bert Moody collection

A feature of the Southampton shipping scene for many years was the Union Castle ships with their lavender coloured hulls, this one, the *Transvaal Castl*(32,697 gross tons) was built by John Brown & Company on Clydebank and made her maiden voyage from Southampton on the 18th January 1962. Th liner did not retain her lavender coloured hull for very long for at the end of 1965 she was transferred to the South African Marine Corporation, being rename *S.A. Vaal* and was then given a white hull. She did, however, remain on the Southampton—South African mail service until September 1977 when th service was withdrawn. The *S.A. Vaal* was then sold to Carnival Cruise Lines of Panama and was renamed *Festivale*. In 1978 she was completely refitte in Japan as a cruise liner and is still in service today mainly operating from Miami. *Bert Moody collectio*

Opposite page top: The French Line's *France* (66,348 gross tons) one of the finest liners ever to serve Southampton The ship was launched on 11th May 1960 by Mme.de Gaulle at the Chantier de L'Atlantique's yard at St. Nazaire The *France* first called at Southampton on 7th January 1962 while on trials, and she made her maiden trans-Atlanti crossing on 3rd February of that year. The 'wings' on the top of the funnels were designed to emit smoke sideway and so prevent smoke and smuts being blown down on to the decks.
The liner operated regularly on the North Atlantic service until September 1974 when, as a result of the Frencl Government deciding not to continue to pay an operational subsidy for the liner, the French Line withdraw he from service and was laid up at Le Havre. In 1979 the liner was acquired by the Norwegian Caribbean Lines being moved to Bremerhaven where she was refitted for cruising and renamed *Norway*. As such she remains i service operating on short cruises out of Miami. *Bert Moody collectio*

Opposite page bottom: Nederland Royal Mail Line's *Oranje* (20,565 gross tons). Completed in 1939, was due call at Southampton on her maiden voyage in September 1939 en route to the Dutch East Indies, but owing the outbreak of war the call was omitted. In 1941 she was fitted out in Sydney as a hospital ship and operate mainly with the Royal Australian Navy, although she continued to fly the Dutch flag.
A triple screw diesel ship, she was returned to her owners at the end of the war and then became a regular visito to Southampton, firstly operating from Amsterdam to the Dutch East Indies. When that service was withdraw she was employed on an Amsterdam, Southampton—Australia service and later a round the world service. In 196 she was renamed *Angelina Lauro* when acquired by Achille Lauro, and underwent a major refit after which sl operated from Southampton to Australia until 1972 after which she was used entirely for cruising. In March 197 while on a cruise, she caught fire at Charlotte Amelie, St. Thomas Island in the West Indies and sank at her bertl She was eventually salved and sold for scrap, although she never reached the breakers yard for while being towe in September 1979 to Taiwan she sank in the Pacific Ocean. *Bert Moody collecti*

The *United States* (53,329 gross tons) made her first appearance at Southampton on 8th July 1952 when she berthed at the Ocean Terminal at the end of her maiden voyage—a record breaking crossing of 3 days 10 hours 40 minutes from Ambrose Lightship to Bishop Rock, a record which still stands today. The return crossing was made in 3 days 12 hours 12 minutes thus gaining the Blue Riband of the Atlantic, which she still holds. The *United States* became a regular

Red Funnel's tug/tender *Calshot*, built in 1930 by John I. Thornycroft & Company at Woolston, Southampton, operated out of Southampton from 1930 until 1964, except for the war years, when she saw service at Scapa Flow and on the Clyde. In 1964 she was sold and renamed *Galway Bay*, being based at Galway, Eire, for local excursion and tender work. Her original steam engines were then replaced by diesel engines.

In 1986 she was acquired by Southampton City Council, and returned to Southampton in October of that year, since when the vessel has been berthed at Southampton Town Quay. It is the intention for the tug/tender to be restored to her original condition as much as possible and to be renamed *Calshot*. She will then form part of the Maritime Museum complex which is being developed in the Ocean Village at Southampton, formerly part of the Outer Dock.

Bert Moody collection

A view of Vospers Shipbuilding yard at Woolston, Southampton taken in 1977 from the then new Itchen Road Bridge, showing the frigate *Constituicao*, one of four Mark 10 frigates constructed by Vosper Thornycroft Ltd. at Woolston for the Brazilian Navy between 1971 and 1977. Also in the picture is a reminder of the past—one of the diesel-powered Floating Bridges, No. 12, also built at Woolston by J.I. Thornycroft & Co. Ltd. in 1964. Shipbuilding has been carried out on the Woolston site for over 100 years; a yard was established there in 1876 by Thomas Ridley Oswald, later to become Oswald Mordaunt. Subsequent builders included Southampton Naval Works Ltd., Mordey, Carney & Company, and J.I. Thornycroft & Co. Ltd. who took over the site in 1904. J.I. Thornycroft & Co. Ltd. was amalgamated with Vospers Ltd. in 1966.

F.R. Sherlock

This book would be incomplete without mentioning the paddle steamers which once graced the Solent. The paddle steamer *Emperor of India* owned by Cosens & Company of Weymouth could be seen in the Solent during the summer months. The vessel was built in 1906 as the *Princess Royal* for the Southampton, Isle of Wight & South of England Royal Mail Steam Packet Company, but as her speed did not come up to contract requirements the ship was not accepted by that company and in 1908 was sold to Cosens. Between the two wars she operated regularly from Weymouth and Bournemouth, and during the Second World War was used as a minesweeper and an anti-aircraft ship. In 1947 a major re-fit was carried out presenting a new appearance as shown in this picture. After 51 years she was broken up in Belgium in 1957. *Bert Moody collection*

Left: The paddle steamer *Whippingham* was completed in 1930 by the Fairfield Shipbuilding & Engineering Company Ltd. at Glasgow for the Southern Railway. She was designed for long distance excursions, which were a feature of the Solent, particularly in pre-war days, but she also took her turn on the Portsmouth—Ryde passenger service as required. A coal burner throughout her life, she was sold for scrap in 1963 being broken up in Belgium. *Bert Moody collection*

Below: Cosens' paddler *Embassy* was formerly the Railway steamer *Duchess of Norfolk* built in 1911 by D.W. Henderson & Company Ltd. for the joint fleet of the L&SW Railway and the LB&SC Railway. As such operated on the Portsmouth—Ryde service until 1937 when she was acquired by Cosens for excursion work and renamed *Embassy*.

During the Second World War the vessel served as a minesweeper and an anti-aircraft ship under the name of HMS *Ambassador*.